THE HARD WEATHER BOATING PARTY

I0139713

Naomi Wallace

BROADWAY PLAY PUBLISHING INC
New York
www.broadwayplaypublishing.com
info@broadwayplaypublishing.com

Cover art by Bruce McLeod
First printing: October 2014
I S B N: 978-0-88145-590-8
Book design: Marie Donovan
Page make-up: Adobe Indesign
Typeface: Palatino
Printed and bound in the U S A

THE HARD WEATHER BOATING PARTY was
commissioned by Actors Theatre of Louisville.

The play was first produced by Actors Theatre of
Louisville in 2009 as part of the 33rd annual Humana
Festival of New American Plays. The cast and creative
contributors were:

STADDON...Michael Cullen
LEX...Jesse J Perez
COYLE...Kevin Jackson

Director..Jo Bonney
Scenic designer.. Paul Owen
Costume designer...Jennifer Caprio
Lighting designer....................................Russell H Champa
Sound designer..Matt Callahan
Properties designer..Doc Manning
Movement consultant .... Delilah Smyth
Fight director .... K Jenny Jones
Stage manager.. Kathy Preher
Production assistant ....Mary Spadoni
Dramaturg .... Adrien-Alice Hansel
Casting.. Vince Liebhart Casting

CHARACTERS & SETTING

STADDON VANCE, *fifty years old, white male*
COYLE FORESTER, *late forties, African-American*
LEX NADAL, *early twenties, Latino*

Time: The day after tomorrow

Place: Rubbertown, U S A

Set: a very sparse, simple Motel 6 room. Two single beds, small desk, lamps.

For Peter Rachleff.
Thank you for your critical support.

For Jerry Tucker,
dear friend and inspiration,
who has always been at our side

ACT ONE

(Rain is heard on the roof of the motel room. No lightning, but steady rain.)

(Lights up on STADDON VANCE, *a quiet, determined middle-management man in his fifties who has worked his way up. He is standing in the center of a cheap, sparsely furnished motel room, staring intently at the floor. He carries a brown paper bag with a liquor bottle and cups inside it. There are two single beds.)*

*(*STADDON *stares for some moments at a small, perhaps foot long, crack in the hotel floor. After some moments, he carefully gets on his knees and tries to see inside it. He looks and looks but he can't really see anything.)*

(Suddenly LEX *bursts into the room. He is a smart, energetic, curious.* STADDON *gets to his feet.* LEX *is dripping wet with rain, but he takes no notice of it.)*

STADDON: You're supposed to do a knock.

LEX: We didn't discuss a knock.

STADDON: You still could have done a type of knock.

LEX: What type of knock?

STADDON: You know. Tap ti tap, tap ti tap ti tap. That kind.

LEX: If you want a tap ti tap ti tap ti fuckin' tap type knock I can go back out and try it again?

STADDON: I was just expecting a knock.

(LEX's boots leave damp prints as he walks around the room.)

STADDON: Lex Nadal, right?

(LEX ignores STADDON.)

STADDON: Mister Nadal, glad to meet you. In person.

(STADDON holds out his hand, and moves towards LEX.)

LEX: Didn't I tell you to keep your distance?

(STADDON watches LEX)

STADDON: Would you like a towel?

LEX: No thanks.

STADDON: You're making the floor wet.

LEX: Yeah? I do the same to girls so what's the problem? *(Checking out the room)* I've stayed in worse. I've stayed in better. This is O K, isn't it?

STADDON: Yeah.

LEX: When do we start?

STADDON: There's no hurry.

LEX: I'm ready now.

STADDON: That's good. But we have to wait until midnight, at the least.

LEX: I'm ready now. *Estoy listo.* [I'm ready.]

STADDON: Well. I appreciate that you have arrived ready.

LEX: Where's the other guy?

STADDON: He should be here any minute.

LEX: You better hope so. *(He now takes off his cap and wrings it out over the trash can, then puts it back on)* You ever wondered 'bout the bed covers?

STADDON: They're in every motel, no.

LEX: Sort of quilted, slippery and ugly.

STADDON: Your point?

LEX: They're made to withstand staining. Rubs right off. Lot of staining in motels. And there's always a big mirror so that you can… Hey, where's the mirror?

STADDON: Room service took it away.

LEX: Why?

STADDON: A distraction we don't need.

(LEX *clears his throat and spits on the floor. Then he lightly touches his hand to his stomach for just a second, as though it hurts him, but then he's fine)*

LEX: You're sure you want to do this, right?

STADDON: Of course.

LEX: 'Cause, it was your idea—

STADDON: We're going to do it.

LEX: Because you called me. Yeah. You dialled my number.

(STADDON *now notices the spit on the floor)*

STADDON: Is that yours? *(He means the spit.)*

LEX: Not anymore.

STADDON: Please. Clean it up.

(LEX *just stares at* STADDON *as he steps on the spit and slowly drags his foot across the floor, smearing it away.)*

LEX: Done, boss.

STADDON: Tonight we're equals.

LEX: Said the zookeeper in his crisp new suit. What's your first name *(Beat)* Mister Staddon?

STADDON: Staddon is my first name. Vance is my last name.

LEX: Vance. That's kind of a. Loser name like Nance. Anything that rhymes with chance hasn't got one.

STADDON: Have a seat, Mister Nadal. Relax.

LEX: No thanks. But you can call me Lex. If you don't over do it. *(He sees the crack in the floor.)* Mierda [Shit.] You bust the floor?

STADDON: No. No, I did not.

LEX: Motel guy is gonna be pissed.

STADDON: It was like that when I arrived.

LEX: They make you pay for stuff when you break it. I'm not paying.

STADDON: We didn't do it so let's forget about it.

LEX: You hear that?

STADDON: What?

LEX: Shhhh.

(LEX puts his ear to the crack and listens. A rhythmic knock on the door. LEX jumps up. STADDON walks to the door. The knock comes again. STADDON opens the door, and lets COYLE in. COYLE is in his forties, brilliant but reluctant to display it; both cynical and romantic at the same time. His hands are partly numb, and sometimes don't work exactly right. But COYLE is used to it and most of the time can camouflage the problem.)

STADDON: *(To LEX)* Now he did a knock.

COYLE: Vance?

STADDON: Yes. Staddon Vance. Come in.

(COYLE comes in warily. He looks around the room, then at LEX. COYLE has a raincoat on. It's dripping wet.)

COYLE: This the other guy?

LEX: Lex Nadal.

COYLE: Looks like a kid.

(LEX *gives* COYLE *the finger*)

COYLE: So the circus has arrived. *(He removes his rain coat.)* Damn. I'm feelin' better tonight than I have in months. Blood's movin', muscles jumpin'; Hey, something's not right about this room... Where's the mirror?

STADDON: The motel took it back.

COYLE: But I might want to have a look. Before we start.

STADDON: You look just fine, Mister Forester. I can tell you that. Mirror won't.

COYLE: Only two beds. We're not sleeping here, right?

STADDON: No, we're not.

LEX: Motel guy doesn't know that.

COYLE: Yeah. Three men, two beds. I mean. You know.

LEX: We can share, old man. I always like meat in my bed, no matter the grind.

COYLE: Hey. You watch your step.

(STADDON *opens the paper bag and takes out a pint of whiskey and three plastic cups.*)

STADDON: Mister Nadal, Mister Forester. Party of three. That's us. Let's toast.

(STADDON *parcels out the cups, pouring a little whiskey into each one. The men make a toast, using the plastic cups. But no one knows what to say. After an awkward silence,* LEX *speaks.*)

LEX: Here's to this "bang" changing our lives—

COYLE: Here's to gut rot courage, and no cop outs—

STADDON: Here's to us. Amen.

LEX: I don't do Amen.

COYLE: I don't either. Most of the time.

STADDON: Well. All right. Why don't we just say "Hurrah"?

(The men nod at one another.)

COYLE/LEX/STADDON: Hurrah!

(Uncomfortable, they drink and look into their cups. Then LEX dives onto the bed to try it out.)

LEX: Not bad. New springs.

COYLE: So what did you bring?

STADDON: A turn of phrase. Or two.

COYLE: That won't cut it.

STADDON: You'd be surprised. Properly placed it can bring a man to his knees and melt his caps. I also brought a gun.

LEX: A gun. Cool.

COYLE: And a bullet, I hope.

LEX: Very cool. Like January. February.

STADDON: Of course.

LEX: Winter's best 'cause it hurts less in the cold.

COYLE: That's for sure. Summer's are a bitch. And August the hottest bitch of all.

(LEX whips out a knife.)

LEX: I brought a knife.

COYLE: That's a kitchen knife.

LEX: So?

COYLE: To chop vegetables.

LEX: Isn't that what we're doing tonight?

STADDON: Put the knife away, Lex. You might cut yourself. A gun is enough.

LEX: You sure?

STADDON: I'll let you know if we need it.

(LEX *puts the knife away.*)

STADDON: You're from Algonquin Parkway?

COYLE: Born there too.

STADDON: *(To* LEX*)* And you?

LEX: Wilmouth Ave.

COYLE: You don't live in Rubbertown.

STADDON: No. Across the river.

LEX: Like to keep your distance.

COYLE: It rainin' on your house tonight, Vance? In *(Emphasizing)* Clarks-ville?

STADDON: Of course it is. We all get the rain.

COYLE: What's it like in your neighbourhood?

STADDON: It's—

COYLE: clean.

STADDON: It's—

LEX: quiet.

STADDON: It's—

COYLE: Safe.

STADDON: I was going to say it's got trees.

LEX: Like a forest in Rubbertown. That's what is used to be.

COYLE: It was never a forest.

LEX: Big trees up and down the streets. You could swing from one branch to another and make it all the way round the block.

COYLE: The Big Boys always live 'cross the river in Clarksville.

LEX: You're at Amalgamated?

STADDON: There's nine industries in Rubbertown. I've worked at six.

COYLE: Why you move around so much?

STADDON: Restless.

LEX: You don't seem like the restless type.

COYLE: Started at Amalgamated when I was nineteen. Still there. Take my eyes out I could walk every room backwards in that building and not touch the walls.

LEX: I started at D-Chem. Switched to Amalgamated two years ago.

STADDON: Why?

LEX: Piss breaks. You get piss breaks at Amalgamated. Not at D-Chem.

STADDON: You have a bladder problem?

LEX: If I did it'd be none of your business.

STADDON: Fine by me.

LEX: Hey. You don't know me so don't even think about my bladder.

COYLE: Then why you keen on piss breaks?

LEX: There's other things you can do on a break.

STADDON: Ah. Smoke!

LEX: Screw.

STADDON: No one fornicates at our plants, on our time.

LEX: There's sixty-four tanks at Amalgamated, at any one time half of those are empty.

COYLE: Like rooms, yeah. Empty rooms.

LEX: What do you think people do with empty rooms?

STADDON: Just stories.

LEX: And the tanks are sound proof.

STADDON: We're not stupid.

LEX: Yeah?

COYLE: Okay. Okay. Let's focus here. *(To* STADDON*)* You've got the information, time, place?

STADDON: Yes.

COYLE: One man.

STADDON: One man.

LEX: Then the money.

COYLE: What if his family gets in the way?

STADDON: One at a time then.

*(*COYLE *watches* STADDON *some moments.)*

COYLE: Tell me something: why tonight?

STADDON: What do you mean?

COYLE: Why not yesterday, or the day before?

STADDON: Well. They've forecast snow. It should be a beautiful night. The kind of night to take your breath away.

LEX: To take someone's breath away.

COYLE: But why'd you call me?

STADDON: Because you've got it in you.

COYLE: Bullshit me and I'll take your teeth. You don't even know me.

STADDON: I knew you'd say yes.

COYLE: How?

STADDON: I don't know. Perhaps a look. A way of walking.

COYLE: We never met.

STADDON: I've seen you at work. You don't hesitate when you walk, Mr. Forester. Once you put your foot down you commit to the direction. No matter what that direction is.

COYLE: Huh. And him? *(About* LEX*)* Why'd you bring him in?

LEX: He called me 'cause he needed me. *(To* STADDON*)* Didn't you? You needed me.

STADDON: Yes. Yes I needed you. Both of you. There are some things a person can't do alone. You need. The company of other men.

LEX: Zookeeper needs the seals.

COYLE: You be careful; I'm no seal.

*(*LEX *barks like a seal. He barks at* COYLE. *Then* COYLE *barks like a seal, and it's believable, and much better than* LEX'*s seal. And he's aggressive with his bark. Even scary.* COYLE'*s seal shuts* LEX *up.)*

LEX: *(To* STADDON*)* What about my walk?

STADDON: I didn't notice your walk.

LEX: Then why am I here?

STADDON: It was in April. Just after lunch break. I saw you hit your locker.

COYLE: So the boy's got a temper. Girlfriend burn you?

STADDON: Twenty nine times you hit that locker.

COYLE: Damn.

STADDON: It's a wonder you can still use your hands. I saw in you, Mister Nadal, a man who doesn't quit 'til he's broke.

LEX: I wasn't broke, the locker was.

STADDON: Exactly what we need.

COYLE: Hey. Cut the sweet talk. You know what sticks in my throat? Lex and me. Okay. We work the same floors. But you. Why?

LEX: Yeah. Why?

STADDON: It happened to all of us.

COYLE: You were always at a distance.

STADDON: Not lately. Actually, I tried speaking with a couple of co-workers.

COYLE: White folks.

STADDON: Managers.

COYLE: That's what I mean.

STADDON: Not all of them are—

COYLE: Ugly. Right. But most of them are—

LEX: White.

STADDON: Some of them are—

LEX: Assholes.

STADDON: Not all of them are white.

COYLE: But most of them are ugly.

STADDON: I don't care about ugliness.

LEX: Well, you wouldn't, would you?

STADDON: Not all of your co-workers are—

COYLE: ugly. No, they're not. And some of them are white, too. But none of them live in Clarksville.

STADDON: But the point is that some of the managers are black. Asian, even.

COYLE: How many?

STADDON: At Amalgamated? One.

LEX: Black. Or Asian?

STADDON: Portuguese, I think.

COYLE: *(Shaking his head)* Right.

STADDON: The point is, with the mangers, I couldn't even get the conversation going. So I asked both of you, you said yes.

COYLE: The lower depths... They're an easy lay, right?

STADDON: We don't have to like one another to work together towards a common goal. As a unit.

COYLE: We are not a unit.

LEX: We're three separate pieces.

COYLE: That don't fit.

STADDON: Liking one another is not necessary. What we need is agreement as to the basics. So, let's talk about the plan. Lex, what are your thoughts?

LEX: I think we need to bust right in there. Because I know how to bust, I volunteer. *(He acts this out.)* I'll run at the door with my shoulder. I'll do a side-winder-power-run the last few steps and then Bang. Ker-pow. Smash, splinter, splinter. The door breaks open and we're in.

STADDON: I have a key.

LEX: Oh.

COYLE: You ever kill anyone, Lex?

LEX: I don't think so.

COYLE: What the hell does that mean?

STADDON: I have not.

LEX: *(To* COYLE*)* Have you?

COYLE: I'm a fucking vegetarian. No.

STADDON: So that's why we have to talk about it. This is an extraordinary endeavour. This is not "I'll have a burger and fries". This is not "cash or credit". This is a detour.

COYLE: A one-way street.

STADDON: Lex, what's your proposal once we're in?

LEX: I'm going to kick him. *Lo voy a patiar y patiar.* [I'm gonna kick him and kick him.] Just like the door. Kick, kick, kickaroo.

COYLE: He might kick back.

LEX: Not after my kick.

COYLE: A man's head is hard. Thick.

LEX: I'll put velocity behind it.

COYLE: You sound eager, Lex?

LEX: I'm tired. That's a kind of eager without the sleep.

STADDON: Kicking is a possibility. Absolutely a possibility. But it takes too long.

COYLE: I could choke him. I got the grip.

STADDON: Choking is more focused than kicking.

LEX: *¡Chingao!* [God damn it.] You're favouring Coyle.

STADDON: I'm not favouring anyone. We're trying to decide, together, what's most efficient. We could use the gun. Unfortunately we don't have a silencer.

COYLE: Then it will be loud.

LEX: Loud but quick.

STADDON: Perhaps I should repeat myself: I made it very clear on the phone. Whatever we do, we do together. This is not the act of a lone assailant.

COYLE: Look, we go in there together and whoever does the job, does the job.

STADDON: No. Absolutely not. We need something more synchronized. In concert.

COYLE: What the fuck's it matter how we do it? I don't trust you.

STADDON: You can trust me completely.

COYLE: Said the manager. Huh.

LEX: Okay. Here's a plan: I'll kick him while Coyle, you choke him and Staddon you put the bullet in his head. Then we get the cash.

STADDON: Hmmm. Yes. That might be the only way that we can do this together, in the actual moment. But we must also speak to him before he dies. Each one of us. One at a time. And then we must give him a chance to speak.

COYLE: What the hell is this? A fucking twelve step murder program?

STADDON: Don't you dare. (*For the first time he loses his cool, but regains it quickly.*)

COYLE: What?

STADDON: Say that word among us.

(COYLE *eyes* STADDON, *unsure.*)

COYLE: Hell?

STADDON: No.

LEX: Fucking?

STADDON: No.

COYLE: Murder?

STADDON: Not again. Not among us. It's a degrading word. It degrades us.

COYLE: The "M" word?

STADDON: It's godforsaken. We are not.

COYLE: Right…

LEX: Chill Vance.

COYLE: But why do we have to let him talk?

LEX: The man's had years to talk. His talking is done. When I'm spending his money, that'll be his chat.

STADDON: It's important that a man knows why he's to die, exactly. We must allow him to gather his thoughts before he dies. And I want the last thing that goes through his mind to be us.

COYLE: Yeah. All of us.

STADDON: Thank you. Thank you both.

LEX: *(Casually)* I'm going to be sick.

COYLE: *(Casually)* Don't do it on the floor.

(LEX sits on the bed and dry heaves into his open hands, as though he might catch whatever comes up. But nothing comes up and he recovers. The others are hardly bothered.)

STADDON: "But thou wilt sinne and grief destroy;
That so the broken bones may joy,
And tune together in a well-set song,

LEX: Huh?

COYLE: Full of his praises,
Who dead men raises.
Fractures well cur'd make us more strong."

LEX: Double fuckin huh.

COYLE: George Herbert.

STADDON: I'm impressed.

COYLE: Shit. You disappoint me, Staddon. You can't picture a black man reading nothing but a summons, can you? Bedside reading. Like most of us, I don't sleep. So I read in the night.

LEX: I don't read at night. I pretend I'm asleep.

STADDON: Well Chelton Steff will not be asleep, though he'll surely be a-dying. And after we've allowed his last thought, we'll shoot a tiny round window straight through it.

COYLE: And then get the hell out.

Coyle/Lex/Staddon: Right.

Lex: I hear it's a rush, killing a man. Like a water cannon pumping through you, te levanta [it lifts you], lifts you right off the ground. That's what I heard.

Coyle: Bullshit. You're making it into something it's not: magic show, pick a card. Fuck that. It's flushing the toilet. It'll feel good after you let it out.

Lex: You know, we're talking about doing it together, this. Thing, this killing thing, and I hardly know you guys. You're almost strangers. Coyle, I've seen you at work. I think we've sat next to each other in the cafeteria.

Coyle: You did a chicken and peel at lunch. You wrapped your piece of chicken in a banana peel.

Lex: Yeah. That's me. Chick 'n 'Nana. My invention. You should see how it works in the bedroom.

Coyle: (To Staddon) But we never sat with you. You eat in your office.

Staddon: I share a. Cubby. With two other people. I don't do lunch. I munch on saltines when I'm hungry.

(Some moments of silence. Lex and Coyle stare at Staddon. He gets uncomfortable)

Staddon: What?

Lex: (To Coyle) Did he say 'munch'?

Coyle: Yeah. I think he did.

Lex: I can't work with a guy who uses that word.

Staddon: What's wrong with it?

Coyle: Munch is not to be associated with food. We don't munch.

Lex: We open up the craw and—

STADDON: *(Interrupts)* All right then. Let me rephrase it: I…snack on saltines…when I'm hungry.

COYLE: Snack.

LEX: He did it again.

COYLE: *(To LEX)* Should we go on home?

LEX: Snack? Sounds like something pathetic you let loose in the toilet.

STADDON: Listen. I don't care about these words. Snack. Munch. We are planning a

LEX: Murd—

STADDON: Don't say it.

LEX: We are planning a mmm—

COYLE: —munch.

LEX: —a snack.

COYLE: We are planning a munchy snack.

LEX: And we'll put our feet up on his desk while we eat it.

STADDON: *(Interrupts)* Stop it. You are disrespecting me. We cannot work together if there's disrespect. We need to be a unit.

COYLE: I don't do units.

LEX: Neither the fuck do I.

STADDON: Fine. Not a unit then. But we have to co-ordinate this. Like a team.

LEX: I don't do teams.

COYLE: Me either. Uniforms are ugly. I like to dress nice.

STADDON: Fine. Okay. Then what shall we call our… club?

(COYLE and LEX both think it over.)

COYLE: How 'bout the "Lets-get-this-yellow-bastard-of-a-night-over-with-so-I-never-have-to-see-either-of-your-duck-fuckin-ugly-faces-again" club. Now munch on that.

LEX: Hey. You like me.

COYLE: Just cause we sat at lunch together doesn't mean I'd slap your back if you were choking.

STADDON: I'd slap your back, Lex.

LEX: Yeah? Thanks. I could make you a Nana and Peel.

STADDON: I'd love to try one.

(LEX *smirks at* COYLE)

COYLE: Could we get started?

STADDON: It's too early. We have to be sure he's in bed. Asleep. We need to relax.

LEX: I don't want to relax. I want to move.

COYLE: Let's watch some tv then. Nothing else to talk about. Where's the T V?

STADDON: I had it removed.

COYLE: Already making decisions without us.

LEX: Yeah...

STADDON: We must have some quiet before this. Endeavour.

COYLE: That's not the point. Point is you didn't ask us if we wanted it removed.

LEX: You didn't count us in.

STADDON: You're right. I should've asked you. I will now. Coyle, do you want me to call room service and order another T V?

COYLE: I don't watch T V. I just like the weight of it in the room.

STADDON: Lex?

LEX: I don't care. But I might get bored. And that smells bad.

STADDON: All right, then it's decided; we're okay without the tv.

COYLE: And the mirror. You decided that one too.

STADDON: Do either of you want me to retrieve the mirror?

COYLE: You know, something 'bout this whole night don't feel right.

STADDON: You said you were feeling better than you have in months.

COYLE: That's my point exactly.

(COYLE *approaches* STADDON *menacingly.*)

LEX: Hey. Hey. No mirror, no tv. We all agree. Party of three, right?

STADDON: That's right, Lex. Party of Three.

COYLE: Sure. But if we got an hour to spare then leave me alone. Call me when it's time.

(COYLE *throws himself on the bed with a small book and begins to read. He has a slight problem turning the pages.* STADDON *watches him)*

STADDON: *(To* COYLE*)* I get the distinct feeling you don't like people.

COYLE: "Like" people? I wouldn't do folks that kind of harm.

(STADDON *continues to watch* COYLE. LEX *finds a way to amuse himself.)*

STADDON: I didn't choose you because of your stride, Mister Forester.

COYLE: *(Continues reading)* Hear that, Lex? He lied. Knew we couldn't trust him.

STADDON: I saw you reading in the canteen. You got up from the table to get an extra helping of peas.

COYLE: See how they watch us? Tabs on our peas. Tabs on our piss.

LEX: Tabs when we jerk off in the bathroom.

STADDON: You do that at work?

LEX: Come and have a look see at noon. Stalls are full.

STADDON: I didn't know that. You see, I don't know everything. But I did see Coyle get up from the table to get that extra helping of peas.

LEX: I fucking hate peas. Little green sneaky bastards travel in a crowd.

STADDON: *(To* LEX*)* He used a knife for a book mark. I opened to the page he was reading:

LEX: I got an idea. So there's no T V.

STADDON: "Hard as hurdle arms, with a broth of goldish flue/ Breathed round; the rack of ribs—"

LEX: But that don't mean we can't do some entertainment. Coyle. Truth or Dare.

STADDON: Deeply religious, he was.

COYLE: Nah. That was his mist. He's all about "Amansstrength", or lack of it.

STADDON: A strange and brutal style. He forced the disparate together.

LEX: Staddon. Truth or dare?

STADDON: That day I thought: a man who can read Hopkins without sentimentality, that's the man I need.

COYLE: I'm as sentimental as a butterfly, asshole. Why do you think I'm here?

LEX: I'll say this one more time, then I'm going to hit someone:

(COYLE *now looks at* LEX.)

LEX: Truth or dare. *(Beat)* We'll pass the time. Break the ice.

COYLE: There is no ice.

LEX: Yes there is. I'm cold just standing next to you two frozen motherfuckers.

COYLE: No.

LEX: Why not?

COYLE: Leave me alone. *(He continues reading.)*

STADDON: Wait a minute. Just minute… Should we play his game? Yes. Let's play Lex's game.

COYLE: It's a kid's game.

STADDON: Sure. But it's a bonding exercise. It builds trust. We'll need that tonight. We'll need that tonight more than anything else.

COYLE: More than the gun?

STADDON: Yes. More than the gun.

COYLE: I forgot how to play.

LEX: *(Delighted)* Okay. I say "truth or dare", let's say, to Staddon here. Then he has to pick. If he says "truth", he's got to answer any question I ask him. Honestly and in detail. If he says "dare", he's got to do what I ask, no cop outs.

COYLE: What if he refuses?

LEX: Then we…kill him?

(COYLE *and* LEX *laugh*)

LEX: But he can't refuse. That's the trust part. That's the core. I go first?

(No one objects.)

LEX: Coyle. Truth or dare.

COYLE: Ask Staddon first. He wants to play.

LEX: Staddon?

STADDON: Fire away.

LEX: Truth or dare.

STADDON: *(Eager)* Truth!

LEX: Truth. Truth. Let's try and make these questions—

STADDON: Constructive.

LEX: Bonding.

STADDON: Bonding.

LEX: All that. Check.

COYLE: Right.

LEX: Okay… Okay… Okay. *(Beat)* Staddon. Staddon. Staddon.

COYLE: That's his fucking name, Lex.

LEX: Have you ever, at any time, in any place, inserted a hard or narrow instrument into the hole at the end of your dick?

(STADDON is frozen some moments. Then:)

STADDON: How dare you!

LEX: Hold it. Hold it. Just answer the question. Honestly and in your own time.

COYLE: I'm not playing this game.

LEX: Hey. I didn't ask you I asked Staddon. Staddon, should I repeat the question?

STADDON: Yes… Certainly not! I heard you. I heard you. And my answer is no. I did not insert a hard instrument into the hole. No.

LEX: Hard or narrow. What about narrow?

STADDON: I no longer see the benefit to this exercise.

COYLE: Answer the damn question.

LEX: Answer or you break the trust. Break the trust and we could be three dead men tonight.

(After some moments)

STADDON: Yes. Narrow. Yes.

(COYLE and LEX burst out laughing. When they subside, STADDON continues steadily.)

STADDON: But that was many years ago. I just wanted to see if it would be painful.

COYLE: Was it?

LEX: Hey. This is my question. You stay out of it. *(Beat)* Was it painful?

STADDON: At first. But then something interesting happened—

COYLE: That's enough.

LEX: What happened?

COYLE: Stop. And if you think you're going to get a chance to ask me about blunt instruments, you're dead wrong.

STADDON: *(To COYLE)* Truth or Dare.

COYLE: Dare, motherfuckers. Ha!

STADDON: Oh. Dare. I'd rather you say 'truth'?

LEX: No. He can't change it now. You have to make Coyle do something.

STADDON: Do something.

LEX: Yeah. Anything. Just not. Life threatening.

STADDON: All right. Coyle. Coyle Forester. What can I make you do?

COYLE: Whatever it is, yours'll be worse, bud.

STADDON: Dance for us.

(COYLE laughs. LEX and STADDON don't.)

STADDON: Ballet. Yes. Dance some ballet.

LEX: Cool.

COYLE: Out of luck. I can't dance.

STADDON: Ballet. The best you can do will be acceptable, right Lex?

LEX: But it's got to be ballet.

COYLE: I don't know ballet.

STADDON: Make it up.

COYLE: You can't make up something that already is.

STADDON: Do the damn ballet.

LEX: Now!

(LEX and STADDON give COYLE a hard look. They wait. Finally COYLE lifts his arm as though he'll begin. He makes one motion, then quits.)

COYLE: No fucking way.

STADDON: Keep the trust, Coyle.

LEX: Yeah, keep the trust.

(COYLE just glares at the men. He stands in silence some moments. Then he readies himself, doing some boxing moves. Then he does a couple of awkward, stiff poses. Then, he begins to move into a kind of ballet, working to make the simple moves, then moves more advanced. He moves slowly, and somehow painfully. He almost looks ridiculous. He begins to hum classical music for himself now. The other men watch. After some moments, they hum with him. He is really putting his all into the effect. He even attempts a couple of small leaps. The cumulative effect of his dance now loses its ridiculousness, and becomes somehow impressive,

moving. He lastly holds a pose. Then quits. LEX *and*
STADDON *clap.)*

COYLE: Triple fuck you both. Hey. I keep the trust. Let
no man ever say I don't. Ever. *(Beat)* Staddon. Truth or
dare.

STADDON: Ask Lex. It's his turn.

COYLE: I can ask who the hell I want to ask. Right, Lex?

LEX: Right.

STADDON: I won't answer any more questions about
my penis.

COYLE: Truth or dare.

STADDON: Dare.

COYLE: *(Right into it)* Show me how your old man hit
you when you were a kid.

LEX: Smack.

STADDON: *(Calmly)* How did you know he hit me?

COYLE: I didn't.

(STADDON *just nods. He walks over to* COYLE. *He circles
him slowly. Once. Twice)*

COYLE: Took his time did he?

STADDON: Yes. He took his time.

(Suddenly STADDON *throws a quick, hard punch into*
COYLE's *kidney. It hurts* COYLE, *but he absorbs it well)*

COYLE: Son of a bitch.

STADDON: He was. But when I got scarlet fever. Nine
years old, I shook so hard the bed shook too. He held
me 'til my fever broke.

LEX: My turn. Someone ask me.

COYLE: Nah. I quit.

LEX: We all get a turn.

STADDON: *(To* COYLE*)* Do you feel closer to me now?

COYLE: Nope…

STADDON: Bonded?

COYLE: No way.

STADDON: Don't think I do either… *(Beat)* …Coyle. Lend me your book. We'll wait 'til midnight, then we'll go.

LEX: Just one fucking minute. We quit when we're done. We're not done. We're not done! Ask me, Staddon. Truth or dare. Ask me. Ask me.

STADDON: Can't you see we've lost interest?

LEX: Ask me. *¡Pregúnteme horita!* [Ask me right now!] Ask me or I walk out of here.

COYLE: You better ask him.

STADDON: Okay, Mister Nadal. Truth or Dare.

LEX: Both.

STADDON: Both?

COYLE: You can't say "both", you have to choose. You're an idiot, Lex.

LEX: I say both. I'm bending the rules. Bending the rules doubles the trust.

COYLE: Shit. Maybe he's right.

STADDON: Okay, my young friend. Double the trust. *(He winks at* COYLE.*)* I dare you to…sing us a song, while…answering this question: If you were ever to grow up, what would you be?

*(*COYLE *laughs with* STADDON. LEX *ignores them, taking it very seriously)*

LEX: Damn. That's tough.

COYLE: Keep the trust.

LEX: Can I have a minute to plan it out?

STADDON: We'd like it to be spontaneous.

COYLE: Yeah. Shoot from the hip, baby.

LEX: Let me clear my throat. *(He clears his throat, a number of times.)*

COYLE: *(To* LEX*)* You're stalling. *(To* STADDON*)* He's stalling.

*(*LEX *sings his song hesitantly, haltingly, but with real intent and effort. The tune is original and he makes it up as he goes)*

LEX: *(Sings)* If I could grow up, you know what I'd be?
Not a tailor, nor a tinker, but a…wolf of the sea.
If I could grow up,
If I could grow up,
I know this much for sure,
I'd never…wake up.

Because all of these years have been
pickled in tears.
My mother is old, my father in beers…
(Whispers)
Drunk ass.
(Sings)
My sister, my twin: alike, bone to bone.
But she died—fuck you God—and now I'm ever alone.
So if I could grow up, you know what I'd be?
In a grave right beside her
with the cold dirt over me.

*(*LEX *finishes his song.* COYLE *and* STADDON *are silent for some moments.)*

COYLE: I'm sorry about your sister. I didn't know.

LEX: *(Casually)* A few months back.

COYLE: I met her at the company picnic last summer. Nice looking. Laughed a lot. She didn't look like you.

LEX: We weren't identical.

COYLE: She sick a long time?

LEX: I don't know. She wasn't the complaining type.

STADDON: That was a nice song, Lex. You should write it down.

LEX: You think so?

STADDON: Folks live all their lives and never write a song.

COYLE: I never did.

STADDON: Certainly not a song that rhymes.

LEX: I can rhyme. I can do that. Always could. Anybody got a pen?

(COYLE *and* STADDON *search their clothes half-heartedly for a pen. But no pen*)

LEX: I'll write it down when I get home.

COYLE: We might not make it home.

STADDON: You'll have forgotten the song by then. Spontaneous song, it just disappears back where it came from.

LEX: Where'd it come from?

STADDON: God.

LEX: I don't do God.

STADDON: But he gave you a song just now, didn't he?

(LEX *considers this.*)

STADDON: You mean that, about being a man of the sea?

LEX: Always liked water. My mother says as a little kid I used to hide a lot. One day she can't find me upstairs. Downstairs. Then she hears the water, splashing. It's coming from the bathroom. Two years old and I'm

sitting in the toilet. Not on it but in it. Our toilet had
one of those old pull-chains and I'm pulling it and
flushing myself over and over and its spilling out of
the toilet and onto the floor cause my butts stuck way
down in the hole like a plug. Happy as a bee. Yeah I
like the water. Always wanted a boat. Not a big fancy
one just big enough to float the Ohio river.

STADDON: I know how to sail. Used to go with a couple
of friends from work on the weekends. Friends.

COYLE: Where you want to go, Lex?

STADDON: About the only thing we had in common
was our height.

LEX: *(Shrugs)* You can get in a boat and it doesn't
matter. Every direction is straight ahead clear.

*(Suddenly there is a low rumbling, as though something
were moving beneath the floor, as though a tremor passed
through the room. It lasts only a few seconds, then its gone.)*

COYLE: What the fuck?

(LEX jumps out of the way onto the bed.)

LEX: The floor's moving.

STADDON: Shhh. Shhh. Listen.

(They all listen. It is quiet again.)

STADDON: Probably a bad pipe.

LEX: Big fucking pipe.

COYLE: I don't like it.

*(A smaller rumble. They are all quiet, alert, listening. Now it
is silent.)*

LEX: Shhhh.

*(LEX moves stealthily around the room, looking. He stops at
the bedside drawer. He jerks it open. Water sloshes from the*

drawer. He pulls out the drawer and holds it in his arms and looks into it. It's full of water. The men are silent.)

LEX: Its the rain.

STADDON: Yes. Getting in through the pipes.

COYLE: Drawers don't have pipes.

(They are silent some moments)

STADDON: Maybe not. But we've got more important things to think about.

(LEX slowly pours the water into the trash can. Then he replaces the drawer.)

LEX: More important things. Like "mu...mu...

(LEX is pretending he's going to say "murder". STADDON glares at him.)

LEX: Money.

COYLE: Yeah. Money. I'm gonna buy me a...

LEX: What?

COYLE: I don't know.

LEX: What are you gonna buy, Vance?

(STADDON shrugs that he doesn't know or care)

LEX: You're both dead in the head. I can't stop thinking about it cause I'm sure: I'm gonna buy a boat. And if you two don't know where to put your bucks, how 'bout we go in on one together? Three times the cash will get us three times the boat. *(Beat)* Staddon, you in?

STADDON: *(Shrugs)* Why not?

LEX: Yessss. *(Beat)* Coyle? You want in?

COYLE: With the two of you? Never.

STADDON: Three's company. It'll be grand.

LEX: Grand. Yeah!

LEX: You could be the Captain. We'd take your orders. Right, Staddon?

STADDON: *(Playing along)* Ay, Ay, Sir. We'll scrub the deck. And you'll steer us under the stars—

LEX: —to another land where it never hard rains and people

STADDON: —don't munch, or snack but open up their bellows and take it all in—

LEX: —cause it's so damn plentiful. And there is no sickness—

STADDON: —never any sickness. The only fever around is the heat of the day.

(COYLE considers)

COYLE: Why not?

(LEX lets out a shriek of celebration, which then brings on a coughing fit. He coughs hard, and short and as he does so, he brings something up from his chest. It lands on the floor between the men. The three men silently look at the small blob LEX has coughed up. Miraculously, the phlegm begins to smoke. The men watch the trickle of smoke rise.)

COYLE: But no way we're gonna invest in those buy one get one free pieces of shit that float on water cause you beg it to. We'll buy us a classic. Yeah. With craft, chrome hardware, mahogany sides. How 'bout a Cesilde, 1956? Italian made. They put the double "e" in speed boat.

STADDON: So you know boats?

COYLE: Shit yeah. Ohio river's just 'bout in our back yard. Ever since I was a kid I watched them pass by. Money in motion on water, those classics. Herring Gull. Zamora. Panther.

LEX: I don't care what it is, long as it's quick so no one can catch us.

COYLE: If I'm at the wheel, no one will catch us.

STADDON: No one would come after me anyway. I don't have any family. Not even a sister. Or a brother. It's just me. Not married. So no children. I would have liked to have children.

COYLE: Girlfriend?

STADDON: Had one. But I lost her.

COYLE: That's bad. I never lost my wife. Twenty-three years together. One girl, grown up now. Florist in Tennessee. I get flowers on my birthday. Bouquet so big I can't see when I walk, so much in my arms.

LEX: What's her name? Your daughter.

COYLE: Angela.

LEX: She single?

COYLE: Don't think about it.

(The phlegm has stopped smoking now.)

LEX: I bet her hands smell like flowers from arranging all day. My hands. I come home from work. I wash. They still smell like

COYLE/LEX/STADDON: Eggs.

LEX: But if I had Angela's flowers on top of my eggs... When's she home from Tennessee?

COYLE: Leave it.

STADDON: I had a girl a few years ago. Girl? She was my age. She had this way of clicking her teeth together when she was happy. I first met her I called her "Clicker". And let me tell you men, I had her clicking all night some nights. I could satisfy this woman, yes I could. But time passes.

(COYLE and LEX wait some moments for STADDON to continue but he doesn't)

COYLE: But time passes?

LEX: The Clicker?

STADDON: I've always despised that expression: time passes. So why do I use it? There are sayings I've hated all my life and I don't know how they just climb on in my mouth and sit there. Shit there, really.

COYLE: What happened to your woman?

STADDON: She clicked less and less as time. Went on. I heard her last click one night while I was working her hard below the belt to give her some extra fireworks. She'd already had one orgasm.

COYLE: No, no, no, man. Don't say that word.

STADDON: Orgasm?

COYLE: I hate that word. Why they give something so sweet such an ugly name I never understood.

LEX: Orgasm. Yeah. It's ugly.

COYLE: Like a cross between an organ and a spasm. Or an oyster passing gas.

STADDON: May I finish with the orgasm now?

COYLE: Say "come". That's dignified. To the point. So your woman "comes"… Yeah I love that. Women coming. And I like it all over my face, that's my beauty mask. I walk around all day wearing it, smelling her, hearing her sounds.

STADDON: Her clicks.

COYLE: That too.

STADDON: The next morning she said, "Staddon. I'm not in love with you. Never have been, never will be." Then she left.

LEX: Damn. After all the work you put into it?

COYLE: You use your tongue wrong you can kill her love that quick. You got to use the tongue like a bird. And I don't mean some delicate little tweeter—I mean a powerful bird, a crow or a hawk, and you call to her. Flutter that tongue. Flutter it and flutter it and when she gets close you add a hum.

(COYLE *demonstrates a hum. The others try a hum until it matches* COYLE's *in pitch and tone*)

COYLE: That'll put a sputter on your flutter and send your woman straight to mars.

STADDON: Your wife is a lucky woman.

COYLE: Lucks all mine. She's some woman.

LEX: The flutter, huh? I'll give it a try, Coyle. Whens your daughter get home?

COYLE: Don't do that.

LEX: Hey. Just a joke.

COYLE: I never made a joke about your sister.

LEX: That's why you're still alive.

STADDON: If I'd know, Coyle. If I'd only known.

LEX: (*Dreamily*) I've always liked the taste of cunt. First I ever had, I was thirteen. My sister had a sleep over, five screaming girls in sleeping bags all over the living room floor. There was this one girl named Dallas. Funny name. She could talk about the weather like a bioengineer. Sexy. Middle of the night I crawl on my fours into the living room. All the girls are asleep. Dallas has this zipper sleeping bag and the zipper goes all the way round. I start at her neck and I zip down, slow, slow. Must have taken me an hour to get to her waist, on down to her ankles. I crawl up into the bag from her feet. She was asleep. I pushed up her night-gown and touched her with my tongue. Wild and sweet. Knocked the breath right out of me. I didn't stay long, only a couple seconds. *Todavia me hago la pregunta* [I still ask myself now.] I still ask myself now: was she asleep? Couldn't she feel it in her dream?

STADDON: I'd say you violated that girl. Without her consent it's violation.

LEX: I was a kid.

COYLE: You're still a fucking kid.

LEX: After we kill Chelton Steff, you won't say that again.

STADDON: That's right, Lex. That's right. *(He glances at his watch.)* But before we head out, I suggest a little warm-up, so that when we arrive, it will be more manageable. Coyle, you pull him out of bed.

COYLE: He's got a wife. What about her?

STADDON: We'll improvise on her. But the power is Chelton Steff. We go for him first. I'll be Chelton.

(LEX laughs as STADDON unbuttons his shirts and cuff sleeves.)

STADDON: Is it such a stretch? We have to practice. If you want to play piano, you practice. If you want to kill a man, you practice.

(STADDON lies down on the bed, and closes his eyes. The other men just stare at him, unsure)

COYLE: You don't look like Steff. Though Chelton Steff is ugly. How long's he been in Rubbertown?

STADDON: Seventeen years. Came in as top manager, fresh out of Princeton. In just six years, I, Chelton Steff, was running the show. That's how good I am.

COYLE: Yeah, what makes you so good?

STADDON: I make the shareholders money. I keep—

COYLE: —Wages capped.

STADDON: I keep—

COYLE: Unions out.

STADDON: I do what needs to be done.

LEX: But Steff gives us pee breaks.

STADDON: Because I care about my workforce.

COYLE: Yeah, you love us.

LEX: But if we can't keep up. If we fall behind.

COYLE: If we get sick enough that we can't work.

STADDON: Then I send you home.

COYLE: You fire us.

LEX: Never fired me.

COYLE: I keep up. I don't fall behind.

STADDON: I'm at the top. Look up. You can see the soles of my shoes. I'm floating over your heads. I never come down—

(Suddenly COYLE *jerks the bed into the center of the room between him and* LEX.*)*

COYLE: I thought you were asleep?

STADDON: I am. I'm dreaming.

LEX: What are you dreaming?

STADDON: I'm dreaming I'm just a boy again and I'm—

COYLE: What?

STADDON: fishing.

COYLE: Predictable.

STADDON: But with my hands. And I'm in Harrods creek and it's a summer day and I'm wading in my shorts and I reach under this bank and I grab hold and I think its a rock but its moving. I pull it out and it's a water turtle. A little buddy.

LEX: Aw.

STADDON: Not much bigger than a half dollar.

COYLE: I found one of those once when I was a kid.

STADDON: And it's swimming in my hand. There's no water in my hand but that doesn't keep it from trying. And I've never seen anything so strange and. Spectacular.

(Suddenly COYLE *lunges at* STADDON *and drags him violently out of bed and onto the floor.)*

COYLE: And that's when I drag that bastard out of bed. He drops the turtle and the creek smacks him right in the face.

*(*COYLE *slaps* STADDON *a few hard, quick times.)*

STADDON: Yes. Okay. Yes. Just like that. Just like that. And now you, Lex. You start kicking. Kicking and stomping. Stomping and kicking. Come on! Come on!

LEX: I don't want to hurt you, Vance.

*(*STADDON *suddenly jumps up and grabs a chair. He uses it against* LEX, *as a lion tamer would.)*

STADDON: I'm not your amigo, kid. I'm Chelton Steff and I don't give a shit about you.

*(*STADDON *uses the chair to poke at* LEX. LEX *runs away, circling the bed.)*

STADDON: I thought you were ready. Are you ready, Lex? Are you ready?

*(*LEX *finally reacts and viscously attacks the chair. He kicks it and stomps it and breaks it into pieces)*

LEX: Where's your turtle now motherfucker? *(Suddenly he looks around the floor.)* Shit. I didn't step on it, did I?

COYLE: *(Playing it seriously)* Nah. It crawled up under the bed. It's safe.

STADDON: *(Interrupts)* By now I'm almost done for. Coyle is still choking me and Lex has stomped me into pieces.

(The men surround the broken chair, as though it were Chelton Steff)

STADDON: My arm's broken in three different places.

LEX: And your shoulder's popped.

COYLE: And you haven't had a breath in almost three minutes and you're beginning to fade. You're turning blue.

LEX: Grey. You're turning grey.

COYLE: And slobbers coming out of your mouth.

STADDON: Like cottage cheese.

COYLE: Nah, not cottage cheese… Like porridge. Yeah, porridge.

STADDON: Exactly. And that's when I, Staddon Vance, step up and say "Mister Chelton Steff. You know why you're about to die?" And he's an intelligent man so he says "Yes".

COYLE: He even tells us why, hoping that might soften us up.

(LEX stomps on a piece of chair.)

LEX: But we don't soften up.

STADDON: We say, "Make your last thought a good one cause you'll be living with it for eternity." And then

COYLE/LEX/STADDON: Bang!

COYLE: You really think we should give a man like him time to prepare a last thought?

STADDON: It's standard decency. No need to be bastards. *(He cleans up the broken pieces of chair.)*

LEX: What'll it be, huh? His last thought.

COYLE: Mine would be…. I don't know. My daughter. My wife.

LEX: Ah, ain't he cute? *(Beat)* So hey, what are our chances?

STADDON: That we get away with it?

LEX: I don't want to die in his home.

STADDON: I'd say maybe a seventy/thirty chance.

COYLE: Let me guess: the seventy isn't the percentage for our escape with the loot.

STADDON: I'm sorry.

LEX: Thirty percent chance we make it out of this night alive, that's good enough for me.

COYLE: We stick to our plan, I'd say fifty/fifty.

STADDON: I appreciate your optimism.

COYLE: They won't get me.

LEX: Yeah. Me either.

(STADDON studies the men.)

STADDON: Good. *(Beat)* Good. I knew I chose right… Gentlemen, are you ready? Coyle, you brought the rags?

COYLE: Yep.

(COYLE takes a crumpled paper bag out of his coat. He throws a mask to LEX and STADDON. Easily, surely, the men put the stockings on their heads. STADDON pulls his stocking completely over his face. They stand in a row, and they no longer look uncertain, but professional and frightening.)

STADDON: This is the kind of moment where prayer comes in handy.

COYLE/LEX: I don't pray.

STADDON: Then lets just…think…how we want it to be. Tonight.

LEX: If you think hard enough on a thing, it can happen.

COYLE: When I was a kid I stared at a fork for three hours, trying to make it bend. Like some guy did on tv. Three hours. And nothing happened. Never did like the look of a fork after that. I still feel it begrudged me.

LEX: Maybe you didn't give it enough kick.

STADDON: Maybe it didn't bend because you did it alone. Now if you put three men together, minds on a fork—

LEX: —something might happen.

STADDON: Three men together, thinking hard on a night—

COYLE: —and anything can bend?

STADDON: Why not?

(The three men consider this, then COYLE *makes up his mind)*

COYLE: All right. Lets do it.

STADDON: Lex?

*(*LEX *pulls his stocking down over his face)*

LEX: *Estoy listo.*

STADDON: Coyle?

*(*COYLE *pulls the stocking down over his face)*

COYLE: Yep.

COYLE/LEX: Staddon?

*(*STADDON *shows the gun)*

STADDON: Gottcha.

LEX: With that son of a bitch's cash, we'll buy us that boat. Rush the Ohio, glide the Mississippi and shoot right out Hell's asshole and on to new waters—

(The room shakes, hard, once, twice. Then there is a long tearing sound and a crack in the floor appears, perhaps three or four feet long, in front of the men. It is in a different place from the first crack. Then it's quiet. The men are motionless, stunned, looking down at the gash in the floor)

COYLE: That's no broken pipe.

LEX: Shit.

STADDON: It's just a crack in the floor.

COYLE: Right.

LEX: Right.

STADDON: It's time to go.

LEX: Yeah, lets fuckin' vamos.

COYLE: Okay. Here's to a quick kill and keeping the trust.

(COYLE puts his hand out, then LEX puts his on top of it, then STADDON puts his hand on top of LEX's. All three men are now eager, ready.)

COYLE/LEX/STADDON: Hurrah!

(Black out. In the dark the crack in the floor glows blue like water. Again we hear the sound of rain.)

END ACT ONE

ACT TWO

(Same motel room. The rain has stopped. LEX *is standing poised with an oar over his head. It is a long, beautiful, wooden oar.* LEX *is performing impressive, though original, martial arts-type moves.)*

(A rhythmic knock comes at the door. LEX *freezes at the sound of the knock. The knock comes again. Then* STADDON *opens the door and enters. Now* LEX *continues his moves.* STADDON *watches* LEX *perform with the oar. He says nothing for some moments.)*

STADDON: *(Slowly)* You have an oar.

*(*LEX *concentrates further on his moves.)*

STADDON: You look good with that oar, Lex. Not every man looks good with an oar. *(Beat)* Where's Coyle?

*(*LEX *doesn't respond)*

STADDON: There's blood on your face.

*(*STADDON *moves to clean the blood off* LEX*'s face.* LEX *brandishes his oar to protect himself, but continues his moves.)*

STADDON: It's different now, Lex. Everything is different.

*(*LEX *ignores* STADDON.*)*

STADDON: Did you see that dining room? Wow. You could park a half dozen fire trucks in that room and still have a ball. Water taps like chandeliers. How is it possible for a man to get a bathroom like that? Rooms like that? 'Cause he's Top Dog for seven chem plants in the neighbourhood. King of Rubbertown. Chelton Steff.

(*On hearing Chelton Steff's name,* LEX *quits his moves.*)

LEX: I never even saw him before tonight. Slept with his socks on.

(LEX *begins to laugh.* STADDON *approaches him and spits on his hand. Now* LEX *lets him clean the blood off his face.*)

LEX: Fucking idiot. Slept with his socks on!

(STADDON *quits cleaning* LEX's *face.*)

STADDON: I sleep with my socks on.

LEX: You ever met him before tonight?

STADDON: Not personally. Once or twice a year they'd bring a dozen of us to the office, pep talk, glass of juice.

LEX: When he bled, I felt nothing. When I saw his socks I. His socks had little trees on them and we're not close to christmas.

(LEX *gets a sudden sharp pain in his stomach.* STADDON *studies* LEX.)

STADDON: You hear that? (*Beat*) Rain stopped.

LEX: (*Listens*) Yeah?

STADDON: It won't last.

LEX: I used to look forward to rain. Can't hardly remember what its like to see a dry sidewalk. All we get is— (*He winces again.*)

STADDON: Rain. (*Beat*) How many times?

LEX: We said we wouldn't talk about it.

STADDON: I'm just asking.

LEX: You mean how many times at work?

STADDON: Yes. At work.

LEX: Five times.

STADDON: More than that. I'm certain.

LEX: No. I'm certain. *Estoy seguro.* [I'm certain.]

STADDON: Alright. But I'd still say seven... No. I'd say eight times. That you know of.

(LEX *stares at* STADDON, *surprised.*)

LEX: Huh. *Hijo de puta.* [Son of a bitch.] You're pretty good. Yeah. Eight times. How'd you know?

(STADDON *shrugs*)

LEX: What about you?

STADDON: Guess.

LEX: No way I could guess.

STADDON: Try.

LEX: I'd say three. Maybe even just. Two.

STADDON: Wrong! Twice early on. Eleven times in the past eighteen months. Thirteen contamination episodes.

LEX: No way, no way.

STADDON: Yep.

LEX: You don't rinse reactors, regulate exhaust.

STADDON: I got you beat!

LEX: You just count our peas.

STADDON: Thirteen.

LEX: Really?

STADDON: Cross my heart *(Beat)* They'll come for us, you know. In a little while they'll figure it out and they'll come for us.

LEX: *(Quietly)* Days?

STADDON: No. Hours. Maybe less.

(*Suddenly* COYLE *bursts into the room, out of breath, but excited*)

COYLE: We did it. Jesus, we did it!

LEX: (*Whoops*) Yes we did! I tied him to the chair.

COYLE: And I hit him—bang—so he'd stop jumping.

LEX: Did I kick him before I tied him to the chair or afterwards?

COYLE: Both. You did both, Lex.

(LEX *barks like a seal.* COYLE *matches it.*)

LEX: His nose bled when I slapped him. He was sweating. What a stink. Like he'd been in an onion shower.

COYLE: When I gave him my fist, you hear that air go out of him? (*He makes the sound of air going out of a tire.*) Just like a tire.

LEX: You got a punch, Coyle. Jesus, you weren't lying.

COYLE: And you got the kick, brother. Just like you said.

LEX: (*Hopefully*) I think I broke my foot.

COYLE: The wife was more calm.

LEX: I like lines on a woman's face.

COYLE: But he wouldn't open the goddamn safe.

LEX: No fucking money to take home. I'd counted on that.

COYLE: And that damn alarm. My ears are still ringing.

LEX: I thought we disabled it.

COYLE: There must have been two.

LEX: But that didn't stop us. Nothing could've stopped us.

COYLE: I'm running and I'm running and I'm hearing the sirens and the cops are getting close and my chests about to burst. Damn. I feel like I'm seventeen again.

(COYLE shadow boxes with LEX. LEX responds. They go at it hard, almost hitting each other but not quite. They feel exhilarated.)

STADDON: I'd just like to point out to you both that I'm the one who actually pulled the trigger.

(The men stop shadow boxing.)

STADDON: Not you, or you.

COYLE: Yeah. But we did it together. Just like we said.

LEX: Just like we said.

(COYLE pours them each a drink.)

COYLE: Here's to a job well done.

LEX: I second that.

STADDON: Here's to both of you. For showing up in the first place. For keeping the trust.

COYLE: And. Reluctant as I am to say it: Here's to Staddon Vance—

LEX: Ex-zookeeper—

COYLE: —for calling us here together. For making this night the only night in a fucking long line of nights that matters.

LEX: I second that.

STADDON: Thank you. Thank you both. I'm touched. Here's to all of us. Men in hard weather stick together. To our Party of Three.

LEX: To the Boating Party.

COYLE: There's nothing else like it!

COYLE/LEX/STADDON: Hurrah!

(The three men drink. Still high with the event. COYLE *goes for another drink but trips over the smaller of the two cracks in the floor.)*

COYLE: Shit. It's worse. *(He examines the crack. The he rolls up his sleeve and starts to put his hand down inside)*

STADDON: Don't do that.

LEX: You could get electrocuted. Don't.

*(*COYLE *slowly puts his hand in the crack, then squeezes his arm in. It's deep. He pulls out his arm; his arm and sleeve are wet.* LEX *is upset.)*

COYLE: Maybe the basements flooded.

STADDON: A motel room has a basement?

*(*LEX *observes the water dripping from* COYLE's *arm, like blood.)*

LEX: Thats how he was bleeding. His nose. Dripping just like that. Oh God. We killed a man.

*(*LEX *vomits into his hands but nothing comes up. Dry heaves)*

COYLE: Yep. We killed a man. So don't call on God, Kid. Cause God just stopped coming.

STADDON: You said you quit God.

COYLE: Yeah, but sometimes on a Tuesday or maybe a Thursday it comes into me, maybe it's God, I don't know. But I do know this: when you take a motherfucker out, God steps back. Nothing can cross that divide.

LEX: The Chair. We'll get the chair.

STADDON: Yes, we will.

LEX: Well I'm going to stay in this room. Fuckin' cops'll have to kill me.

COYLE: I never been shot before.

STADDON: If they call my name. If they say "Staddon Vance. Come out with your hands in the air," I'll do it. If they call my name I'll have to. *(Beat)* Coyle, you with me?

COYLE: Bullshit. I step outside with you, it's me that's dead.

STADDON: I wouldn't let that happen.

(STADDON throws COYLE a hand towel. COYLE's hands seem to be more numb now and he has difficulty drying himself off. STADDON observes this.)

COYLE: Cops take one look at us and think—

LEX: —you're both ugly.

COYLE: Yeah, but guess which one they're gonna think killed Steff?

STADDON: Coyle. There's something I'd like to know.

COYLE: Don't ask me.

STADDON: You don't know what I'm going to ask—

COYLE: *(Interrupts)* Yeah I do.

LEX: He asked me too.

STADDON: *(To COYLE)* How many times?

COYLE: What difference does it make?

STADDON: Because it happened to all of us.

COYLE: Huh.

STADDON: How many times? Please.

COYLE: Shit. That I know of?

STADDON: It is always. Only ever. What we know of.

COYLE: At work? Or at home? Cause I have no idea how many times it happened when I was home. I stopped counting.

LEX: At work.

COYLE: Guess.

LEX: Seven.

STADDON: No. Give me a minute. You've lost some feeling in your hands, right?

(COYLE *gives* STADDON *a look.*)

STADDON: Yes, I can see it. And the whites of your eyes, have a hint of blue. Almost.

LEX: You can figure out his hands by his whites?

STADDON: Just something you pick up on after a while. *(To* COYLE*)* And your feet are hot.

COYLE: As a son of a bitch.

STADDON: I oversaw the workforce on level three through seven for years...I'd say you were exposed to general concentrated chemical contamination at the workplace...nine times. Exactly.

(COYLE *eyes* STADDON *a moment.*)

COYLE: I started in the warehouse, loading, unloading tanks. Then moved on to flushing pipes, mixing gas, cleaning stacks. Last couple of years I replace damaged equipment, gauge tank levels. *(Beat)* You're right. Nine times of "accidental" exposure. That I know of.

LEX: I never got out of flushing pipes. Six years and still flushing pipes.

STADDON: *(To* COYLE*)* But you don't cough.

COYLE: No. I don't.

STADDON: But that strange. It's a typical symptom.

COYLE: What is this? Fucking doc time? Because I made it clear from the start, that I don't like to talk about the symptoms—

LEX: *(Interrupts)* Hey! Hey! They're coming for us. Any minute now they'll break through that door. We just going to stand here? Run! Should we run?

STADDON: We wouldn't get far. You know that.

LEX: Then it's any minute now. Any minute. *Cualquier minuto, cualquier minuto.* [Any minute. Any minute.]

(LEX points the oar at the "door", chanting "any minute.")

COYLE: *(To distract LEX)* Where'd you get the oar, Lex? Nice looking oar. But we'll need two oars to row.

(LEX quits chanting.)

LEX: Steff had only one on his wall. So I took it. Didn't get the money but we got an oar.

STADDON: That's a museum piece.

LEX: Yeah?

COYLE: There's a plaque on it.

(LEX looks on the oar and finds the plaque.)

COYLE: What's it say?

LEX: *(Reads, unsteadily)*
"I want to be a cavalryman
And with John Hunt Morgan ride,
A colt revolver in my belt
A sabre by my side.
I want a pair of…

LEX/STADDON: …epaulets

(STADDON finishes the quote for LEX.)

STADDON: …to match my suit of gray,
The uniform my mother made
And lettered `C S A'."

COYLE: Huh. C S A. Confederate State Army. Glad we wasted the asshole.

LEX: Who's John Hunt Morgan?

STADDON: Confederate Army general who led his army a thousand miles to cross the Ohio as he tried to invade the North. Oar belongs to the Morgan's Men Association.

COYLE: Yeah, but Morgan failed, the slave owning snake, took his sorry ass back through Kentucky to Bardstown. *(To STADDON)* How do you know about the Morgan association?

STADDON: I was their secretary.

(COYLE moves in on STADDON.)

COYLE: You confederate bastard.

STADDON: No. A few hundred dollars a year to keep their papers in order. I was a good paper keeper. There were only three members listed. But there were hundreds of associate members. Of course, folks like that, they want their names kept out.

COYLE: My old Kentucky home.

LEX: I'm going to crack some cops with this oar if they get close enough.

COYLE: I don't think Morgan would appreciate that. Now take a whack at me and the old gizzard might show his ghost!

STADDON: I couldn't stand the chanting. They would stand in a circle and chant that song. Bank men, real-estate men, company men. *(Chants)* John Hunt Morgan. John Hunt Morgan.

LEX/STADDON: John Hunt Morgan. John Hunt Morgan

(STADDON breaks off the chant while LEX continues quietly to chant the name, using it as music with his oar "moves".)

STADDON: It crawled into my ears like an ear wig and it wouldn't let go. I couldn't sleep at night so after a few months, I quit.

COYLE: Good for you. *(To* LEX*)* Lex. Shut the fuck up.

(LEX *goes quiet*)

COYLE: *(To* STADDON*)* Or I'd have to suspect you of being part of something worse.

STADDON: What could be worse than what's acceptable?

LEX: What are we going to do? What the fuck are we going to do?

STADDON: I'd say we have two choices: we can wait for the cops to find us here, or try and get home to say good-bye to our families.

COYLE: We'd never make it. They'll be combing the streets. You take out one of the most prominent citizens of Louisville and no cop sleeps.

STADDON: Might be worth the risk to say good-bye. Coyle?

(COYLE *doesn't answer.*)

STADDON: Lex?

LEX: I'm staying here. I'll fight it out. Besides, no one to go home to. Pops died in April. Mom just after that.

COYLE: Shit.

STADDON: I'm sorry, Lex.

LEX: *(To* COYLE*)* What about you? You gonna say good-bye to your wife?

COYLE: We did that almost two years ago. When she left.

STADDON: You said you never lost her. You lied.

COYLE: Yeah. I lied.

LEX: What, she didn't want to stay around and change your diapers?

COYLE: I asked her to leave. Then I told her. I gave her no choice.

LEX: Hard man. Hard. Or had you gone soft? That happens too. I can pump mine for hours and it just sleeps.

(STADDON *looks towards the window and speaks slowly.*)

STADDON: In a few hours it will be morning. I'm sorry we're going to die today. It's snowed most of the night.

LEX: You know that's not snow.

(A moment of silence)

LEX: But that's what we tell ourselves when it falls on our roofs. On our sidewalks.

COYLE: Only it doesn't come from the sky it comes from the stacks.

STADDON: A clear sky would be a more kindly day to die in.

COYLE: Sure. When was the last time you saw a clear fuckin' sky?

STADDON: I'd have liked a son to say good-bye to. "Son. I've got to say good-bye." "Son. Son." How beautiful it sounds.

LEX: I'll be your son. If you want to say good-bye to someone.

COYLE: Christ.

STADDON: No. That's not right.

LEX: Why?

STADDON: You're not my son.

LEX: So? Out of all the sick bastards that work at the plant, you chose me. I owe you one.

STADDON: But it's a lie. I don't lie.

LEX: I do. All the time. But at least I'm honest to myself about it.

STADDON: Lying is wrong.

LEX: Lying is a tool. If a screwdriver won't work, try a hammer. If a hammer won't work, try a lie. If it works, use it. *(Beat)* Hi, Pops!

STADDON: I wouldn't know how, really, to speak to a son.

LEX: I'll show you how.

STADDON: Why?

(LEX ignores the question and plays a "son".)

LEX: Hi, Pops! You wanted to see me?

(After a moment)

STADDON: Yes.

COYLE: Jesus.

LEX: What's up, Pops?

STADDON: Pops.

LEX: Yeah, Pops. What's up, Pops?

STADDON: You know I've asked you not to use that name: Pops. I don't like it.

LEX: Why not, Pops?

STADDON: It sounds. Insignificant. I'd prefer it…son…if you'd call me: father.

COYLE: No one says father anymore. These days its Dad, Daddy, Poppa, Hey you, or asshole.

LEX: So what's up *(Beat)* father?

(A slight tremor of joy goes through STADDON)

STADDON: Well. Son. I know we haven't had a lot of time lately, me being at work so often, late home at night. And I know we haven't always seen eye to eye. But—

LEX: *(Interrupts)* Father. My buddies are waiting outside. I gotta go.

STADDON: Wait. I need to tell you something.

LEX: And I need to ask you something.

STADDON: Yes. Ask me. By all means. What do you want to ask?

LEX: Fifty bucks. You promised me fifty bucks for my birthday.

STADDON: When was your birthday, son?

LEX: You always forget. You always forget.

(STADDON *gets out his wallet.*)

STADDON: I'm sorry. I'll give you seventy.

(LEX *takes the money and pockets it.*)

LEX: Thanks, Dad.

STADDON: Dad. Dad. Yes, Dad is all right. But son.

LEX: Yes, Dad?

STADDON: We may not see each other again. We need to say good-bye. Son.

LEX: *(Matter-of-factly)* Shit. You in trouble again, Dad? You been hitting Mom again?

STADDON: Of course not. I never hit your mother.

LEX: You hit me.

STADDON: I never hit you.

LEX: *(Calmly)* You fucking did, Dad. Yeah, for years. Sometimes I'd be asleep and you'd smack me in the head while I lay on my pillow. Mom says it's because you're white and you can't understand. Understand what? You hit Chrissy too.

STADDON: Chrissy…I have a daughter too! A daughter!

LEX: Had. Had. Chrissy's dead. Or did you forget?

STADDON: No. No. I didn't forget. My son, my daughter. My darlings.

LEX: You never loved us.

STADDON: How dare you! I loved you all my life.

LEX: Bullshit. *(He starts to turn away.)*

STADDON: Don't go yet. Son. I'm sorry if I. Hit you. I'm sorry for Chrissy too. Fathers should cherish their children.

(LEX just stares at STADDON. Some moments of stillness. Then COYLE bursts out laughing. The laughter is a release for him. LEX is silent. STADDON seems wounded and retreats.)

COYLE: *(To LEX)* That was good. Yeah, you're good.

LEX: Who you need to say good-bye to, Coyle?

COYLE: I done my good-byes. Now its just me and alone.

LEX: You touch your wife with those hands?

COYLE: Lex. I'm not Staddon. I got a limit.

LEX: A limit. Yeah. I got eight exposures. You got nine. Hot feet. Check. Dick dead. Check. Numb hands. Check. I figure your back teeth are gone. Can't keep food down anymore. Your ears bleed at night? You should see my pillow. Strawberry jam with the pulp. But what's the worst for you, Coyle? What was it that made you send your woman packing?

COYLE: I'll hit you.

LEX: Let me guess. She wouldn't let you touch her anymore cause your fingers are dead.

COYLE: Shut you're mouth, Lex.

LEX: No blood in the tips anymore. Ice.

STADDON: Lex. Don't.

LEX: The wife lay down besides you and you were winter in her bed.

(COYLE *just stares at* LEX. LEX *moves closer to* COYLE, *now speaking gently*)

LEX: What was her name?

(*For some moments* COYLE *is silent.*)

COYLE: It took years on that work floor to happen. First, I lost the memory of my feet. As though grass and my toes never happened or dirt, or fuckin' wool socks. Then I lost the memory in my hands. The feel of water. Gone. The weight of a glass. Gone. (*Beat*) Her name? (*Beat*) Coralee. (*Beat*) Know what I regret? That I didn't kiss her good-bye. If I'd touched those lips again, I wouldn't of let her go. First time I met this woman was like doin' 90.5 on the freeway, rolling down the window she just pours all over me. That kind of rush makes you go from little bitty breeze inside you to a cataclysmic storm. That strong. (*Beat*) But now I can't remember kissing her. Can't remember the feeling. The memory of her kiss is wiped out. (*To* STADDON) You say Hopkins forced the disparate together. Forced. You're wrong about him, Staddon. The right word is fused. Hopkins fused the disparate together, like they were meant to be together. Belonged together. Like my woman and me.

STADDON: Like the three of us?

(*The men eye one another for some moments.*)

LEX: When I was a kid and pissed off at Mom or Pops, I'd go to my room and I wouldn't come out. My sister Chrissy, to cheer me up, she'd put little notes under my door that said stuff like "There's a turtle in your head," or "Why can't you stop thinking about groundhogs?"

And soon as I read her note sure enough I'd have a
turtle in my head or I couldn't get the groundhogs out
of my skull. Chrissy wouldn't go to the hospital. She
knew they couldn't save her. She lay adying five days.
I held her hand. Then she said, "*Mátame.*" [Kill me]
She could hardly speak. "*Mátame*". I said no. She kept
saying "Kill me." She was in.

COYLE: Unimaginable pain. So you killed her.

LEX: I didn't kill my sister, the fuckin' industry did.
We never closed the windows in our house. We knew
it did no good. The sirens. The release. The sirens. The
release. Seems like somethings always getting loose in
Rubbertown. Getting broke. Getting spilled. Into the
air.

COYLE: How'd you do it?

LEX: How many times were we fuckin' poisoned and
we didn't know?

COYLE: Lex.

LEX: Her fingernails had fallen off. She wept at how her
hands looked. She'd always been proud of her hands.
And it hurt when I held her hand but she wanted me to
hold her hand. I'd put applesauce on her tongue. The
only thing she'd stomach in the end. In the end. That's
a stupid fucking phrase cause the end doesn't come
when it's. Love.

COYLE: Just tell us.

LEX: *Mi mejor amiga.* [My best friend] She was my best
friend. My twin.

COYLE: How did you kill her?

LEX: *(Explodes)* Shut the fuck up. ¡*Cállate el pinche osico!*
[Shut the fuck up!] You don't know. You don't fucking
know— *(Now he is quiet again)* —what happened. If I'd
killed her she wouldn't have died. If I'd killed her she

wouldn't have died. Like that. Her mouth full of. Her lungs full of. Blood. She didn't blame me for what I couldn't do. And all I could do was sit beside her. They killed her. Then I killed her again by not killing her. So twice. Twice she had to die. Cause I was too scared to do it.

(The men are silent.)

COYLE: You know what I thank God for Staddon? I thank God he let us kill Chelton Steff. Motherfucker fought and won every lawsuit we brought against him. For every scientist our neighbourhood brought in to fight him, and let me tell you it cost us, he had three brought in to do a ring dance round our graves. The industry says we're dying 'cause we use too much barbecue sauce on our ribs, use too much grease in our pans. Lawyers say we don't get enough exercise. Mayor assures us we're just a sick people. But little by little spring doesn't come anymore to Rubbertown, summer neither. No leaves on the trees so autumn don't bother. Even the calendar's sick. No more seasons. Just rain, and night.

(After some moments)

STADDON: I didn't kill Chelton Steff.

(COYLE and LEX just stare, stunned, at STADDON.)

STADDON: I put the gun to his head. I said: Hello. My name is Staddon Vance.

COYLE: You didn't kill him?

STADDON: My name is Staddon Vance and I work for you.

LEX: You didn't fuckin' kill him?

STADDON: I'm your third sub manager at Amalgamated Synthetics.

COYLE: But I heard the shot.

STADDON: I can take you for a tour of your site.

LEX: I heard it too.

STADDON: As you very well know, we run a tip top ship.

COYLE: I don't believe you.

STADDON: He didn't speak.

LEX: He's lying, Coyle.

STADDON: Then I said "Think your last thought now Mister Chelton Steff because you are going to die."

COYLE: Staddon.

STADDON: I thought he'd say "Eat me, Vance." I thought he'd say "Go to hell, you loser."

LEX: *(Louder)* Staddon!

STADDON: I thought he'd say, "You're a dead man, Staddon, just like me."

COYLE: *(Still disbelieving)* I don't believe it.

STADDON: But you know what he said? He said.

LEX: Tell us you're lying.

STADDON: Chelton Steff said. *(Beat)* "Please please please please please... (*He says "please" an exact number of times, perhaps twenty three times, dead pan, counting, slowly, steadily, then cuts off.)* Exactly that many times. He deserved to die. But in that moment I hated him too much. Killing a man with that kind of hate inside you is a kind of touching. I didn't want to touch him. So I shot him in the leg.

LEX: Jesus. Jesus.

STADDON: He passed out. I ran.

(COYLE grabs STADDON by the collar.)

COYLE: We should do you right now, Staddon.

STADDON: Go ahead. I'll be dead in a few weeks anyhow. It's been blood for a month now.

COYLE: We really should kill you.

STADDON: I'm a manager. I work for Chelton Steff.

(COYLE *pushes* STADDON *away, otherwise he'd hit him.*)

COYLE: So do I.

LEX: Not anymore we don't. Now we don't even have a job. *(Resigned)* Never count on the fucking zookeeper.

(*Suddenly, seemingly out of the blue,* LEX *strikes* STADDON *with the oar.* STADDON *crumples to the floor.* LEX *stands over him.*)

LEX: You promised me. You said it was pay back!

(LEX *begins to beat* STADDON *with the oar as he speaks.* COYLE *turns away.* STADDON *hardly struggles but attempts to curl up and ward off the blows. Then* LEX *pounds the bed with the oar*)

LEX: This was your fucking plan. You told us it was a good plan. It was gonna be grand. We were gonna buy a boat. Coyle was gonna be Captain. We were gonna get away. Now everything is fucked and we've got nothing. Nothing. *Nada. Nada. Nada.* [Nothing. Nothing. Nothing.] *(Then he quits.)*

COYLE: For years, months, you see the end coming. You see your neighbours die around you. *(To* LEX*)* You see your family die too. *(To* STADDON*)* And then you finally do something that your gut's telling you is wrong but feels so damn right. And even if its only for a minute, everything inside you. Lights up. Like it lit up tonight. And now? Just like Lex says. We got nothing. And worse, we've done nothing. I'd wipe my feet on you, Staddon Vance. I'd wipe my feet on you right now but there's a door mat outside I'd rather use.

(STADDON *composes himself before he speaks.*)

STADDON: Well, I can't blame you for drawing the conclusion that it's my fault. *(Beat)* But you walked away, both of you. I was alone.

COYLE: *(To* LEX*)* I knew I should've looked when he did him.

STADDON: But you didn't look, did you Mr. Forester? You walked away. I understand that.

COYLE: So my stomach was flipping. I just stepped outside.

STADDON: And you, Lex Nadal, you ran out to the yard.

LEX: I had to shit. I didn't want to. Not in his house.

STADDON: We went in there. Me, you and Lex. But then you left me to do it alone. Both of you.

COYLE: All you had to do was pull the trigger.

STADDON: Then why didn't you do it? *(To* LEX*)* Or you? I offered the gun to both of you but you wouldn't take it. Neither of you would take it.

COYLE: It was your gun.

STADDON: But it was our pact!

LEX: I kicked him. It was your job to shoot him.

COYLE: I tied him up. I hit him. That's what we agreed.

STADDON: No. We agreed to do it together.

COYLE: And we did it together. We each had our part.

LEX: Yeah. We each had our part.

STADDON: We practised. Before we went we practised to kill him together. We built the trust. We built the trust and you broke it.

COYLE: No.

LEX: You broke it. You broke it.

STADDON: Both of you walked away. I was left alone. *(Beat)* The fact is, you're cowards. And there's nothing worse than cowa—

COYLE: Don't you dare or I'll crush you where you stand.

LEX: Hit him, Coyle. Hit him. He didn't do the job. He broke the trust. He broke the trust. He broke the trust. Hit him. *Pégale. Pégale.* [Hit him. Hit him.]

(COYLE moves in to hit STADDON. LEX continues saying "Hit him" in Spanish, over and over. Suddenly COYLE turns on LEX.)

COYLE: *(To LEX)* Shut the fuck up. You kicked him? You kicked Chelton Steff? Like a fucking ten year old kicks his bedroom door.

LEX: Coyle?

COYLE: You're a bad joke, Lex. You're just a kid.

LEX: ¿Soy un pinche niño? [I'm a fucking kid.] I'm just a kid. Yeah. Then what do you call what you did to him? You're hands were shakin' so hard you couldn't even tie the ropes. I had to do it for you. Pathetic.

COYLE: Shut your mouth.

LEX: Fucking pathetic. Knock the wind out of him? He didn't even have to catch his breath when you punched him.

(COYLE gut punches LEX and it's hard. LEX shuts up. The men are silent now for some moments.)

STADDON: Well. *(Brightening)* He did get a bullet in his leg.

LEX: Yeah. Maybe he bled to death.

COYLE: He'll probably limp for the rest of his life.

LEX: He'll always have a hobble.

STADDON: He won't ever forget us.

COYLE: No. He won't ever forget us.

(A moment of silence)

STADDON: What happened tonight, you gave it meaning. Both of you.

COYLE: Why?

STADDON: Because the industry was killing you with the exposures.

LEX: But you said you wanted to kill him because of your exposures. Eleven times in Eighteen months. That's more than us. Or were you lying? He was lying.

STADDON: No. I wasn't lying. Twice it was an accident when I was on the floor. Then nine times more. I climbed into the tanks. Before they were washed down. Over a period of months I climbed into the tanks and just. Breathed.

COYLE: You mother fucker. You did it on purpose? On purpose? We spend years dodging and ducking what can never be dodged and ducked and you do it on purpose? Why?

STADDON: I saw. I saw your faces over the years. You went in to those buildings and you went in whole. You went in strong like a thousand blocks of ice, hard and clear and useful. Whole crowds of you. Whole crowds. I was outside that crowd. I was outside that. Power.

COYLE: You wanted to join us?

STADDON: Yes.

LEX: So you'd be like us?

STADDON: Yes.

COYLE: Well if that isn't the most disgusting, distorted, sentimental piece of solidarity bullshit I have ever heard. Well, I got news for you Staddon Vance. You are not like us.

STADDON: Now I am.

COYLE: No, buddy. You'll never be like us.

LEX: Cause you had a choice about the exposures.

STADDON: But it brought us together. Like tonight.

COYLE: It won't ever be the three of us.

LEX: Hey. If Chelton's not dead, maybe the cops won't kill us.

COYLE: Don't count on their grace.

(Some moments of silence)

STADDON: You're right. You're both right. I broke the trust. *(Beat)* I'm sorry. I appologize.

(The men refuse to look at STADDON. *Then* STADDON *coughs lightly into his hand. Then he begins to cough and cough and it turns into an ugly cough, as though his insides are coming up. Blood pours into his hand.* COYLE *and* LEX *now glance at* STADDON. STADDON *wipes the blood from his lungs on his shirt. There's a lot of it.* STADDON *composes himself.)*

STADDON: Excuse me. It's all the excitement. Usually I can control it.

COYLE: Well, well, well. *(He slowly begins to remove his shoes.)* So he's not dead. Chelton Steff's not dead. Chelton Steff lives on!

(Now COYLE *reclines on the bed. Then, his feet begin to smoke.)*

LEX: Fucking Jesus Christ.

*(*STADDON *and* LEX *examine* COYLE's *smoking feet.* STADDON *gives a long whistle of admiration.)*

STADDON: I've never seen that symptom before.

LEX: Wow. Anyone got some marshmallows?

(COYLE *gives* LEX *a warning look, but he's proud of his smoking feet.*)

LEX: Hell. I'm hot inside too. Like now, if I swallowed an egg whole it'd be hard boiled in three minutes. But I never been as hot as you, Coyle. *(Beat)* But you ain't all that. You ain't all that! Watch this. Now it'll take a minute cause I got to go in deep...

(LEX *readies himself to cough up something deep. He works and works at it. Lots of noise and effort. Finally he coughs up something into his hands, then drops it on the floor. It's larger than before. It glows florescent.*)

STADDON: Now if that doesn't make you believe in the existence of God...

COYLE: Looks like water from the lake. Same glow. So damn glorious, that lake in the dark. Incandescent, just like Rubbertown at night, like some blow-back acropolis. Smoke, steam, pouring out the stacks—

STADDON: —like Hell's mind on overflow.

LEX: I still swim in that lake. So thick with chemicals you can scoop the water up and pour it like sand. And if I'm not dead tonight I'll swim it tomorrow 'cause its our fuckin lake. Swimming in that lake I feel alive even when its killing me 'cause it's my way of saying fuck you to Chelton Steff.

STADDON: They'll still come for us. Even though we didn't kill him. Attempted murder. They'll still come.

COYLE: Attempted murder. Huh. I'd call it wilful, what they've done to us.

LEX: *(Sings)* If I could grow up, you know what I'd be? Not a tailor, nor a tinker, but a wolf of the sea.
(Speaks to COYLE *and* STADDON*)* I like this song.
(Sings) If I could grow up.
If I could wake up.

STADDON: Coyle. I had one real job in my life to do, and I couldn't do it. I just couldn't do it. And what's worse, maybe I'm glad.

COYLE: Yeah. Maybe we're all glad.

(LEX nods in agreement.)

STADDON: Mister Forrester. I'm dying every minute.

COYLE: Well so am I. So is Lex. It's only months, maybe weeks we got left.

STADDON: I can't do the rest of the minutes. I need you to help me.

LEX: How come you ask him, not me?

STADDON: *(Not looking at LEX)* I can't ask you. You're my son.

(LEX doesn't answer but nods, almost imperceptibly. STADDON puts the gun on the bed but COYLE won't take it. STADDON kneels beside the bed.)

LEX: Shit.

STADDON: I always wondered what would be my last thought when I die? A thought about God? About my baby's clicker? Something bigger than them both?

COYLE: Nah. Don't think I can do it.

STADDON: Yes you can.

COYLE: *(To STADDON)* Shoot your own damn self. *(He walks away.)*

STADDON: But I'm asking you to do it.

LEX: Well don't fucking ask him.

STADDON: But we're friends. After tonight.

COYLE: We're not friends.

LEX: We don't even like you.

STADDON: *(To COYLE)* I need. Your kindness.

COYLE: That's not the kind of feeling you can force.

STADDON: Try.

LEX: Stop it, old man. Just quit.

STADDON: I don't want to die alone. I most likely will if you don't help me.

COYLE: No.

STADDON: But what if I can make you. Remember. Your wife.

COYLE: What?

LEX: Jesus, he's lost it.

STADDON: Coralee. What if I can make you remember her the way you want to remember her?

COYLE: You can't do that. It's gone.

STADDON: Yes I can.

COYLE: You can make me remember?

LEX: He can't. He can't.

STADDON: Yes I can.

LEX: What, like bending a fork? Hey, let's think on my fist, tight as a ball. *(He holds up a tight fist in front of* STADDON.*)* Think on it to open up, Staddon. Think… Think… Pray…all of us together, focus on my fist… *(His fist begins to open, unfolding, as it does it he gives the finger to* STADDON*)* Hey…it works.

COYLE: I can't help you, Staddon.

STADDON: But if I could make you remember her, Coyle, you'd owe me. Right? Keep the trust.

COYLE: You broke our trust already.

LEX: That's right.

STADDON: Then give me a chance to restore it.

COYLE: You're out of your mind.

LEX: No one can do that.

STADDON: *(To* COYLE*)* I can. One chance.

COYLE: No.

STADDON: Close your eyes, Coyle. *(Beat)* Go on.

(To his own surprise, COYLE *closes his eyes.* STADDON *steps towards* COYLE *and takes* COYLE'*s face in his hands.* STADDON *kisses him. For a second* COYLE *resists strongly but then for some moments gives in to the kiss.* STADDON *steps back.* COYLE *turns away, but is so surprised he is calm)*

COYLE: No way, no way.

LEX: Can't you see he's fucking with you?

COYLE: Jesus.

LEX: He's fucking with you!

COYLE: I felt it.

LEX: It's not possible.

COYLE: It was her.

LEX: *Por favor, párale. Parale.* [Please stop.] *(To* STADDON*)* How?

STADDON: I don't know.

LEX: This is bullshit.

COYLE: It was Coralee.

LEX: No. No.

STADDON: You think you two are the only ones who can do things or feel things that you couldn't do or feel before? Smoking feet. Blue phlegm. That's nothing. I knew a man at Carbide. He defrosted valves. He was sick for years. Died last month. After the last exposure, he could whistle Skip-to-My Lou.

LEX: So?

STADDON: From his ear.

LEX: How did you make Coyle remember?

STADDON: *(Shrugs)* Maybe... Maybe this kind of contamination, it leaves behind in us...an opening.

LEX: An opening?

COYLE: Capacity where there wasn't before—

LEX: *(Interrupts)* So? So? Shit. You gonna kiss Chelton Steff? Will that make him remember us? *(To* COYLE*)* And you. You gonna set the industries on fire with your feet? *(Beat)* Jesus fucking Christ. An opening? Capacity? We're just cheap tricks. Cheap party tricks. And then we die.

COYLE: But what if there's a way—

LEX: No.

STADDON: What if we could—

LEX: *(To* STADDON*)* After what you pulled tonight you better shut the fuck up.

COYLE: *(To both men)* Lex is right. What does it matter when we can't—

STADDON: *(Interrupts)* Coyle. We had an agreement. I helped you remember. Now be a man of your word.

LEX: *(To* STADDON*)* No. This stops right here.

STADDON: *(To* LEX*)* Lex. My lungs are filling with blood. Don't make me die twice.

*(*LEX *turns away, thinking of his sister.)*

COYLE: What do you say, Lex?

*(*LEX *doesn't answer.)*

COYLE: I think it's truth or dare.

LEX: Yeah. Truth or Dare.

(Long beat)

COYLE: Choose.

STADDON: Truth.

LEX: Make it good, Coyle. Make it good.

COYLE: Would you do the same for me, right now? If I asked you to kill me? *(Beat)* Would you do the same for Lex?

STADDON: I don't want to—

LEX: *(Interrupts)* Just answer the question, Mister Vance.

STADDON: No. I couldn't do the same for you. *(To LEX)* Or you. I don't have the courage.

COYLE: But you ask it of us?

STADDON: Yes.

(COYLE *and* STADDON *now look at one another, eye to eye, a moment.)*

COYLE: Well, at least you're not bullshittin' us. For that, we're grateful.

LEX: Yeah. We are.

(COYLE *picks up the gun.)*

COYLE: *(Quietly)* Son of a bitch. We work for you, Staddon Vance. We get sick for you. And now we've got to put you out of the misery you've made. All right. Get on your knees.

(STADDON *hesitates.)*

LEX: *(To STADDON)* It's O K. It's O K.

(STADDON *gets on his knees.* COYLE *is behind him.)*

STADDON: Yes. *(To COYLE)* Thank you.

(COYLE *pulls the trigger. There's a "click" but no bullet.)*

COYLE: Damn it.

(COYLE *fires again. Another click.* LEX *urges* COYLE *on).*

LEX: If you stop now it'll be worse. Don't stop.

STADDON: Yes. Keep going. I'll think about math.

LEX: Yes, think about math.

STADDON: That's not a bad last thought.

(LEX *kneels in front of* STADDON)

LEX: Math is a good last thought. Now, Coyle!

(COYLE *fires again, just as* LEX *dives out of the way.*)

COYLE: Shit.

STADDON: Or that one I learned in grade school:
(*Recites*)
Long since I hate the night,
more hate the morning.

LEX: Again!

STADDON: Long since my thoughts chase me

COYLE: (*Click*) Fuck.

STADDON: like beasts in forests.

COYLE: Christ.

STADDON: Sir Philip Sydney.

LEX: (*To* COYLE) Concentrate.

STADDON: Yes, concentrate. We're in Motel 6. In the middle of the world.

COYLE: No. I won't do it.

(STADDON *just continues.*)

STADDON: We're at the center of the earth.

COYLE: 'Cause we're still alive.

STADDON: But what ever happened...I ask you, what ever happened to Motel 5?

(*Suddenly* LEX *pulls out his knife and stabs* STADDON *through the back, into the heart.* STADDON *slumps over, dead.* LEX *stands over* STADDON. *There is a long silence, then the rain begins outside again. A crash of thunder, a flash of lighting. The lamps in the room flicker.)*

LEX: We'll be dead soon. Real soon. By the cops or by the sickness. *(Beat)* So let's pray. I don't pray anymore. But./ Let's pray.

COYLE: *(Overlapping at /)* No. *(Beat)* All right. But to who?

LEX: I don't know. To whoever.

COYLE: To whatever. To whatever's got an ear wide enough to take us in.

*(*COYLE *gets to his knees beside* LEX. *They begin to pray some moments beside* STADDON's *body.)*

COYLE: You know, Staddon woulda loved this.

LEX: Yeah.

(They pray. Then at the same moment, they look up at one another and COYLE *nods.* COYLE *and* LEX *reach over and pull* STADDON *between them.* COYLE *and* LEX *prop up* STADDON's *dead body between them. Now the three men are praying side by side.)*

COYLE: Ready?

LEX: Yeah.

COYLE: Lets do it. Hard.

(The men bow their heads low, and pray again. Thunder rolls harder outside. Loud. Louder. Then there is an ear-splitting crash of thunder and a burst of lightning and suddenly the floor of the motel room cracks open and the hull of a boat breaks up through the floor behind the praying men. COYLE *and* LEX *begin to slowly turn around as the rest of the boat appears and comes to rest/land in the motel room. It is a beautiful, classic 1960's speedboat, with wood sides. It seems timeless.* COYLE *and* LEX *are frozen, staring at it. We can now hear water lapping. The hull of the boat is wet and*

streaming with water. As though a lake were below the floor, or water surrounding the hotel)

LEX: Are we dead, Coyle?

COYLE: Not yet.

(LEX slowly gets off his knees and moves towards the boat)

LEX: Did we do this? *(He tentatively runs his hands along the hull, caressing it.)* Wow.

(The boat seems to glow).

LEX: Lets go for a ride, Coyle.

COYLE: Motel guys gonna kill us.

LEX: Fast, far. The three of us. It's our boat.

COYLE: Yeah. *(Beat)* It's our boat.

(LEX, in one easy, smooth motion, sits on the hull. He looks off in the distance, as though he can see the Ohio. Another violent crash of thunder, right above them, and then a sound as though the whole room were about to split open. COYLE looks up, into the storm, welcoming whatever is coming. Then darkness)

END OF PLAY